REAL8

EIGHT REAL PRINCIPLES FOR RELATING IN A HEALTHY WAY

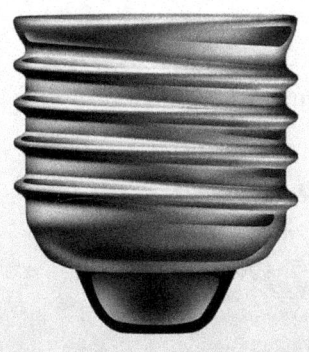

RENETTA S. WATSON

Real8: Eight Real Principles for Relating in a Healthy Way.

Copyright © 2020 by Renetta S. Watson. All rights reserved.

No part of this book may be used or reproduced in any manner whatsoever without written permission except in the case of brief quotations embodied in critical articles or reviews.

Unless otherwise noted, Scripture is taken from the King James Version (KJV), public domain.

For Information, Contact:
RSW Enterprises, LLC
www.renettaswatson.com

Book Creation and Design
DHBonner Virtual Solutions, LLC
www.dhbonner.net

ISBN for Paperback: 978-1-7359648-2-9
ISBN for eBook: 978-1-7359648-3-6

Printed in The United States of America

To Wade...
thanks for being a friend

"Jesus said unto him, Thou shalt love the Lord thy God with all thy heart, and with all thy soul, and with all thy mind. This is the first and great commandment. And the second is like unto it, Thou shalt love thy neighbour as thyself."

-Matthew 22:37-39

CONTENTS

Introduction		ix
1. Principle 1 *Stop the Madness*		1
2. Principle 2 *Know What Causes Relationship to be Unhealthy*		5
3. Principle 3 *Choose Freedom*		13
4. Principle 4 *Understand Why We Were Created & Why Relationships Exist*		19
5. Principle 5 *Beware of the Princess Effect*		23
6. Principle 6 *Your Intent Does Not Always Equate Their Experience*		27
7. Principle 7 *Know the Purpose of Attraction*		31
8. Principle 8 *Love the Way God intended*		33
Final Thoughts		41

INTRODUCTION

A few years back, after having served the community, I had a conversation with a colleague about how the family was being attacked by the subtle deterioration of relationships. That conversation was the start of us relating (establishing a connection, association, or relationship) and lead to many lengthier in-depth conversations.

Out of those conversations came a group, a talk show, a great friendship, and now a book. This book is designed to counteract the attack on the family by sharing some principles to help people relate in a healthy way with God, themselves, and others.

At some point in your life, you experience a relationship that causes you to scratch your head and wonder how in the world did we end up here. You look back, and you go, this was so good. What happened that brought us here? When did this

Introduction

get so unhealthy? Why is this relationship I never thought would end dying? Relationships typically don't become unhealthy overnight, and most are not unhealthy at the start. By the time they become unhealthy, you have time, money, and emotions involved. This is true in all relationship types.

If you are going to have healthy relationships in your life, you must recognize signs of an unhealthy relationship. You must then admit it is unhealthy. You then must decide whether you want to endure the pain of walking away, the pain of staying in it as is, or the pain of working on getting it back to health. Regardless of what you decide, the road won't be easy, but you and your emotional health are worth it.

Although this is a short read, the pages that follow will challenge you to look at relationships differently and ask yourself some tough questions. However, I believe that if you do the work and apply these principles in your life, your relationships will never be the same.

Let's do this!

1

PRINCIPLE 1
STOP THE MADNESS

*Knowledge Without True Intimacy
Makes You an Acquaintance*

Insanity: State of being Mentally Ill; Madness,
Madness: Foolish Behavior

I struggled with putting this principle first. I thought it's probably not a good idea to start a book off confronting the foolish behavior and decisions people make. However, if the rest of this book is going to impact your life, you must look at the statements that follow, examine yourself, and make a conscious choice to change. You cannot have healthy relationships if you continue to move in unhealthy decisions. Below are my definitions of insanity as it relates to relationships.

- Insanity is ignoring the no you need to hear while praying and believing for the "yes" you want to hear.
- Insanity is saying. "God, I trust you," but then doubting that he knows what is and who is best for you.
- Insanity is expecting a man to love you like Christ loves the church when he has never truly experienced the love Christ has for the church.
- Insanity is saying God, "I want your will for my life," while making choices that align with your will.
- Insanity is putting up walls where you did not first set boundaries.
- Insanity is continuing to ask God, "Is this you?" then ignoring all the signs that it's not.
- Insanity is calling someone a friend when they are really an acquaintance.
- Insanity is choosing to pay a high price for what you want instead of freely receiving the gift God wants you to have.
- Insanity is letting another person's need to be healed become the thing that breaks you.
- Insanity is helping or forgiving somebody, then throwing it in their face. When you do that, it was never help or forgiveness. It was collateral.
- Insanity is rejecting the Heaven sent love you

need while holding on to the Hell sent love you want.
- Insanity is rejecting the love of God while embracing a " love " that's hurting you.
- Insanity is backing up from, holding off, and being afraid of what God is doing while quietly suffering as you do nothing.
- Insanity is choosing to pursue the gift (love) you want rather than embracing and enjoying the gift (love) God sent you.
- Insanity is letting a person you know is toxic poison you.
- Insanity is choosing to give the wrong person your trust based on a conversation while making the right person earn your trust based on behavior.
- Insanity is letting a person you know is toxic cause you to become toxic.
- Insanity is mistaking attraction for intimacy.
- Insanity is letting attraction cause you to be intimate with the wrong person and stop you from being intimate with the right person.
- Insanity is stopping at friendship with God when he calls you his bride.
- Insanity is waiting on a prince to become a king while your king is waiting on you.
- Insanity is being blind to the God-sent king right

in front of you while giving yourself to the prince you clearly see.
- Insanity is a king trying to rule a kingdom from a princess perspective.
- Insanity is making a statement when instead, you should be asking a question.

Relating in a healthy way requires us to make sound decisions and operate in a sane way. If you find yourself in any of these statements, choose differently, move forward, and stop the madness.

2

PRINCIPLE 2

KNOW WHAT CAUSES RELATIONSHIP TO BE UNHEALTHY

Never Let the Lens of Your Past Distort the View of Your Present and Hinder the Vision for Your Future!

Obviously, there are many factors that contribute to the breakdown of relationships, and these factors will vary depending on the variables of the relationship. We will just look at a few common factors.

One common factor is that many people bring their past into relationships with them. In some cases, that past hasn't taught them what love is and how to receive love. When this happens, past experiences become filters and lenses through which they see the current relationship; they interpret actions, make decisions, and respond through this lens.

This causes them to deal with people out of impression — an idea or feeling formed without conscious thought and with little to no knowledge. However, we really should be going through the process which enables us to deal with them out of perception (an awareness that forms over time through use of the senses).

We see this played out in the Bible. In the fourth chapter of John, Jesus is sitting at a well and asks a Samaritan woman for a drink. The women immediately began dealing with Jesus out of impression. She says, "Why out of all people, would you ask me for a drink? Your people have nothing to do with my people." Jesus responded by saying, "If you knew who I was and the gift that I am, you would be asking me for a drink."

Continuing to talk of out of impression, she says, "You do not even have anything to draw with. This well is deep; where would this water come from? Are you greater than the person who gave us this well? Her initial response to him was based on her past experiences and what society told her. With no knowledge of him, she decided who he was, what he had, presumed she knew his character, and assumed he would treat her a certain way.

As their conversation continues, Jesus throws her a curveball and tells her to go get her husband. She responds that she has no husband. Jesus said, "Correct. You have had five, and the one you are with now is not yours." This shocking statement causes something to happen. Her senses kicked in, and she became aware of who she was really in the presence of. She said I perceive you are a prophet. Once she perceived who Jesus was, her response was different. Her new response allowed him to unlock and unleash the purpose that was on the inside of her. She began to effectively use what she was previously abusing. A person's purpose in your life can never be fulfilled until you perceive who they are and give them permission to be who they are in your life.

On the other hand, when we deal with people out of impression, we miss out on what it is they are supposed to add to our lives. In addition to this, we tend to focus on the wrong things, often causing us to miss out on experiencing the gift they really are. Even more importantly, dealing with people out of impression causes us not to trust people that we can and should trust.

Lack of trust is another major thing that leads to the breakdown of relationships. Sometimes trust is broken, sometimes it is given to a certain extent, and sometimes it's not given at all. Whatever the case, trust is a foundation relationship, and when it is limited, so is the relationship. Where trust does not exist, a relationship does not exist. The depth of the relationship is proportional to the level of trust in the relationship. A friend of mine said it this way "If I can't trust with the surface of me, I will never trust you with the depth of me."

The Bible speaks of a level of trust most relationships never get to. I call it soul trust. I believe one of the reasons this level is never achieved is because people are unclear about what situations require trust to be simply given and which ones require trust to be earned. This causes them to choose to give the gift of their trust to the wrong people. By the time the right people come along, they have been so hurt they refuse to fully trust anyone else. They end up making Heaven-sent people pay for the actions of the Hell-sent people of their past.

Another reason relationships don't enter the realm of soul trust is we build trust off the wrong foundation. In most relationships, trust is built by conversation but broken by behavior. We talk, we get a "good" vibe, we talk more, and the more we talk, the more we trust. These conversations cause us to build expectations that are often not communicated based on words spoken. We are then disappointed when our uncommunicated expectations aren't met and devastated because their actions don't match our expectations of what their words meant to us.

This brings me to another major reason for relationships become unhealthy, communication. This includes not communicating, under-communicating, over-communicating, and mis-communicating.

Two common areas of struggle are when communicating are expectations and boundaries. When we fail to communicate in these two areas, the result is often feelings of hurt, rejection, and disappointment. Remember this, in relationships, it is likely that pain is an indication that an expectation or boundary has not been effectively communicated.

For example, person A is friends with person B and person C. Person B becomes angry at person C, and they totally disconnect from one another.

Person B believes person A should not have anything to do with person C because they expect their friends not to communicate with people they don't like. Person A believes persons B and C relationship has nothing to do with them and continues to befriend person C.

Person B becomes angry and stops speaking to person A, leaving person A confused and hurt. Person B is also hurt and angry because they trusted person A and now believes they were never a friend in the first place.

WHAT WE SEE HERE IS a classic case of expectations that were not communicated and became the demise of a relationship. If Person A and B had simply had a conversation about their expectations in friendships and set some boundaries within their relationship, this breakdown would not have occurred.

Relating in a healthy way requires having the hard but necessary conversations, which includes dealing with conflict. On the following pages are a few do's and don'ts.

- Do acknowledge that the conflict exists. One of the worst things you can do for a relationship is continuing to ignore issues and sweep things under the rug in the name of peace.

- Do use the 80/20 rule when resolving conflict. Make the resolution of the conflict 80% about the other person and 20% about you. This means they get 80% of what they want, and you get 20% of what you want. If you focus on the other person and the other person is focused on you in the same manner, each person gets 100%. This challenges each of you to see the conflict through the other person's eyes.

- Do fight fair. Remember that conflict is a part of any relationship. In fact, it is how you deal with the conflict that makes the relationship healthy. Fighting in a relationship is not about winning or hurting the other person. If one person wins... you both lose. Fighting in a relationship is about coming to a mutual agreement that's equally beneficial for both of you.

- Don't throw temper tantrums or use manipulation/false humility in an effort to get your way. Not only is this childish, but it's very unhealthy. When you operate in this way, the other person feels used and will eventually leave.

- Don't invite too many people or the wrong people into the conflict. Nothing causes the health of a relationship to deteriorate, like having too many voices in it. You must be very careful about who is in a relationship with you. This is true even in places like work. When you're having issues with your boss, be careful who you invite in. They may be the very person after your job.

Relating in a health way requires us to recognize and acknowledge the signs of unhealthy relationships. We can then decide what steps to take next.

3

PRINCIPLE 3
CHOOSE FREEDOM

Breaking Up is Hard to Do,
But it is Necessary!

You can always tell you are in an unhealthy relationship when you begin to see patterns that mirror the cycle of addiction. When a person is addicted to something, they obsess over it and have a need for it, and choose to continue having experiences with it regardless of the negative consequences. The pattern of addictive relationships looks something like this:

- When you're around the person, you're on a high. You feel good. For a brief period of time, all is well.

- Shortly after you leave their presence, you're still on a high. As the high wears off, reality begins to set in, and you realize as good as this feels to you, it's not good for you.

- Everybody around you knows this relationship is harming you in some way. Some say it; some don't. Either way, you also know this relationship is harming you.

- You decide to walk away. Just when you find the strength to walk away, they call you. They send you that I miss you text. They send a message through a friend. You see or hear something that reminds you of them.

- You start thinking about the good times and how it's really not that bad. You really could do worse. Before you know it, you start looking forward to your next high.

- You start rationalizing and conclude that the pain of being with them is better than experiencing the pain of withdrawal and the reality of being sober. You get high again, and the cycle of addiction repeats itself.

Some people are addicted to the drama of relationships, while others are addicted to the pain. Like any addiction, the longer you use, the more you must use — and the harder it is to break free. Unfortunately for many, it takes hitting rock bottom for them to have a desire for freedom. This does not have to be the case for you! You can choose freedom right now. All you have to do is choose to be free and start making choices that move you toward freedom.

Moving (taking actions that align you're your decision) is essential to your freedom. Remember, a decision not moved in is a decision not made. God makes the way of escape. It's up to you to take it. Below are some ways you can stay free:

- Break up privately before you break up publicly. To accomplish this, you must tell no one about the breakup, not even the other person. You start this process by visualizing yourself being out of this relationship. You then move to looking in the mirror and telling yourself you are out of this unhealthy, unproductive relationship. Tell yourself, "I'm divorcing my past so I can marry my future."

- You then let the other person know of your decision to choose freedom by walking in the freedom you chose. If the relationship is abusive, volatile, or you feel threatened in any way, I highly recommend just showing them. Never intentionally put yourself in a dangerous or life-threatening situation.

- Don't confuse affection and addiction. Like an addiction, affection is a deep, immense feeling. However, affection is gentle, doesn't have negative consequences, and encourages independence. Addiction causes physical and emotional dependence and has adverse effects in various areas of your life.

- Never let another person's actions, thoughts, etc. dictate to you what you deserve.

- Never let someone who does not know who they are to define for you who you are.

- Never put up a wall where there should simply be a boundary. Boundaries are flexible and can be adjusted when necessary. Walls are permanent, and often when put up in relationships, they keep the right person out.

Remember, boundaries were meant to be adjusted, not crossed. When you set boundaries, stay within those boundaries. And, even when boundaries are crossed, most times, the reason they were put there still exists. When that reason no longer exists, you should then adjust the boundary or remove it.

Choosing freedom requires you to get up and/or get clean! Many times, relationships that have addictive patterns involve one of two types of people that create what I call the Doormat Effect. Some people with what I call a "Doormat Personality," and others have what I call unclean feet.

People with doormat personalities tend to love people, love peace, and are very welcoming; they always try to protect people and their feelings. They will usually take one for the team and often take a lot from other people, often without saying anything. They avoid conflict and drama at almost any cost, especially if that cost is to them. Because of their personalities, people expect them to take most things lying down and often make them feel bad when they decide to stand up for themselves. People with this personality must get up, stand up, and walk in their Christ-given identity and authority.

People with unclean feet tend to be people who have not healed from their past, people with low self-esteem, people who are arrogant, people who are overly driven, or people who are just simply mean. These things or a combination of these things cause them to attract or be attracted to people who they can wipe their feet on and walk over. Those with unclean feet must acknowledge the state of their feet, humble themselves, and allow Jesus to wash their feet.

Having clean feet is so important that Jesus told Peter that if he didn't allow him to wash his feet, they could have nothing to do with each other. I believe feet are important because they are designed to carry the weight of the entire body. If the feet are cold, the body is cold because the temperature of the feet influences the entire body. As you walk through life things, attach to you that cause you to have unclean feet.

To demonstrate this, I would like you to take the white sock test. Go clean your kitchen floor. Then put on a white sock. After walking on your clean floor, take off the white sock. If you look at the bottom of your sock, you will see it is not as white as it was. Why? Because as you walked, things attached to your feet. Even the thing you thought was clean had residue from the cleaner that attached to your feet. This is a perfect moment to examine what may have attached to you relationally as you have walked through life and ask Jesus to clean your feet.

Relating in a healthy way requires us to acknowledge toxic, addictive relationships and choose freedom. When choosing freedom, we must walk in it by eliminating the Doormat Effect.

4

PRINCIPLE 4

UNDERSTAND WHY WE WERE CREATED & WHY
RELATIONSHIPS EXIST

Your up-reach affects your in-reach,
Your in-reach affects outreach

You were made for what I call the relationship loop. The relationship loop comes from Matthew 22:36-39. I believe this Scripture is foundational for healthy relationships, covers all types of relationships and all aspects (spiritual, practical, physical, and emotional) of relationships. The loop is God (up-reach), yourself (in-reach), and others (outreach). God is at the center of the loop, and your relationships with yourself, and others should flow out of your relationship with God.

The first two chapters of Genesis reveal to us a model of how and why this loop comes together. First, he created. He had an idea in his mind of something he wanted to accomplish, so he created what was needed to accomplish the thing that he had in his mind.

Next, he equipped us by giving us the tools needed to accomplish what he desired to accomplish. Those tools were his image (a reflection of his nature and character) and his likeness (his ability and authority). Then He blessed them. The blessing is the empowering and grace to carry out the assignment.

This was followed by him giving the instructions be fruitful and multiply. Being fruitful is what you produce and how effective you for the kingdom. Multiplying is how you reproduce and the legacy you leave for the kingdom.

Next, he gave them a purpose. That purpose was to fill and subdue the Earth. This involves natural reproduction and taking care of the place he gave us.

Lastly, he gave an assignment. That assignment is having dominion and is how we accomplish the thing he had in mind.

God created relationships for the purpose of being fruitful, multiplying, and filling the Earth. He wanted us healthy and happy as we fulfill that purpose, so he designed them to benefit us.

I believe one of the reasons relationships become unhealthy is that we have made our relationships more about our benefits and less about his purpose. The problem with that is that benefits are temporary, but purpose is eternal. For example, pleasure is a benefit of sex, but its purpose is for procreation. The benefit lasts only for a certain amount of time. However, when the purpose is fulfilled, an eternal soul is created.

If we are going to relate in a healthy way, we must always remember that every relationship has a purpose and an assignment. Keeping this focus will help us enjoy the benefits of a relationship while not being self-centered and acting as if the relationship is all about us. This is a good time to look at the relationships in your life and ask the following questions:

- Is this a God-sent relationship?
- What is the purpose of this relationship?
- What is the assignment of this relationship?
- What is my contribution to this relationship?
- What is my role in this person's life?
- What is this person's role in my life?

Asking these questions concerning each relationship is the equivalent of putting every relationship in God's care and essential to relating in a healthy way. In some cases, you might night like the answers you get. When that happens, stop the madness and choose freedom.

Relating in a healthy way starts with our relationship with God. If you are struggling in your relationships with yourself and others, this is a good time to examine your relationship with God. Is it where you know it should be? Do you have a relationship with him? If not, today is your day! It's the day you make the best decision of your life. The day you decide to come into a relationship with Jesus! You already have his heart. He loves you so much he gave his entire life for you! The question is, will you give him your heart? If so, say this simple prayer:

> Lord Jesus, come into my heart. I believe you died and rose again for my sins. Today I give you my heart and receive you as my Lord (one who leads and guides) and Savior (one who died for me).

If you prayed that prayer for the first time, I want to connect with you. Please email me at pastorrenetta@yahoo.com.

5

PRINCIPLE 5
BEWARE OF THE PRINCESS EFFECT

*Don't Let Their Fantasy Become
a Reality That's Killing You*

Let me start by saying that although this principle has a feminine name, it can be experienced and displayed by both genders. The name is simply used because when looking at some of the behaviors typically associated with being a princess, it best paints the picture of the concept being conveyed.

Princesses grow up in a world where they want for nothing and believe because they are royalty, everything belongs to them. They are taught kingdom protocol and how to act and behave like a queen, but the mindset and weightiness of the position are often not taught. The result can sometimes be entitled daddy's little's girls with that use temper tantrums to control situations when they do not get their way.

For a woman, the princess effect manifests itself in a scene that looks a little something like this: If you will picture a princess that has been invited to a ball game by a suitor. She arrives at the game in a gown with gloves, a tiara, and a cup of tea. During the game, her suitor offers to get her a bite to eat. She replies I am royalty. I don't need your money. He attempts to explain something to her; she rudely interrupts and says, "I know that." He declines her offer to do something; she replies, "If you love me, you would..." and when that doesn't work, she switches to "Who do you think you are" or "You're trying to control me."

The man displaying the princess effect expects to rule, dominate, and control his palace. He demands everyone caters to him, and everything has to be his way. In most cases, he has nothing to contribute to the home and lacks the skills and wisdom to effectively run the home.

The danger for those relating to those who are dealing with the princess effect is that one can get so caught up in the fun and fantasy of being with a princess that now their fantasy has become your reality. We then end up holding on to the fantasy while the reality is killing us. It is impossible to effectively rule a kingdom from the perspective of a princess because a princess is not mature enough to handle kingdom matters.

Dear King, you do not have to settle for a princess! There is a queen out there mature enough to reign with you.

Dear Princess, there is a king out there wanting you to reign with him. To do this, you simply must be willing to take off your tiara and put on his crown.

Relating in a healthy way requires us to search our hearts and look at our motives for relationships. Are you chasing a fantasy or dealing with reality? Is the fantasy them killing a real you?

PRINCIPLE 6
YOUR INTENT DOES NOT ALWAYS EQUATE THEIR EXPERIENCE

The Best "You" will Never
be Enough for the Wrong Person

Have you ever done something you thought was fabulous for someone and their response was opposite of what you thought it would be and wondered what happened? I have got some great news! Their response may have absolutely nothing to do with you — what someone experiences when they receive from you is likely not based on you.

In fact, it is often based on their impression of you, their interpretation of your actions, and what they believe they know about you. Their impression of you may not be a reality. Their interpretation of your actions is often based on their past experiences or what the experts or people they trust say.

What they know is based on the level of true intimacy they have with you.

Reality is you could be the greatest person in the world, but they will never experience it or see it. Do the same thing for someone with a different perception, interpretation, and knowledge, and they will easily see the gift you are.

On the other hand, their response may have had everything to do with you. Stop right here and ask yourself what do other people experience when they get you? How do you present what you offer? Did you communicate with the other person while creating the experience? Did you give them what they needed/wanted, or did you give them what you wanted them to have? Were your words and actions in agreement? Did you communicate your intent to them?

There can be times when your intentions equate to their experience. This happens when you know a person and are intentional about creating an experience centered around them. Remember, words indicate intent action dictate experience.

For example, I like tulips. A man who gives me roses would be expecting a certain response from me based on the fact society says women love roses. However, if he asked me or got to know me, he would know that I like red tulips. Red roses say I love you. Red tulips say I have your heart.

I love you is used often. It is rare that somebody gives you their heart. It is only when I have your heart that you can love me the way Christ loves the church. Knowing you can love me as Christ loves the church gives me a certain sense of security that allows me to freely give you my heart. You having my heart is what enables me to fully submit to you the way God instructed. You see, a man attempting to create an experience for me would include tulips instead of roses.

Relating in a healthy way requires us to be intentional about knowing those we are in a relationship with. We then use that knowledge in a healthy way that fosters mutual gain and respect.

7

PRINCIPLE 7
KNOW THE PURPOSE OF ATTRACTION

Attraction is Simply a Tool
Used to Bring People Together.

Let's face it — attraction is a part of relating. In fact, regardless of the relationship, the start can be traced to some sort of attraction. Attraction is that thing that draws you to a person. Maybe it is a character trait or interest you have in common. Maybe it is an enemy you have in common. When it is there, it is there. When it is not, it's not. Attraction is a good thing, and I believe when allowed to develop into intimacy, it is a great tool that can assist you in having healthy relationships in all aspects of life.

The issue with attraction is that most people have limited it to be sexual, and therefore it is often used interchangeably with intimacy. Attraction is so much more than that.

Remember, every relationship has a purpose. Attraction is a sense of connection, a drawing intended to bring people together to accomplish a purpose. That purpose may be the creation of life; it may also be the creation of a business or friendship. Whatever the purpose, I believe attraction is a tool God uses to bring us together to relate.

In healthy relationships, attraction causes us to want to know the person and should lead to true intimacy. True intimacy leads to an intertwining of hearts. That intertwining of hearts leads to soul trust. Soul trust leads to productive relationships.

Unfortunately, because we limit it to romantic relationships, it often ends up leading to sex, and the sex gets mistaken for intimacy. When used in this manner, it is easy to confuse the two. Here is how you can tell the difference. Attraction satisfies the flesh intimacy satisfies the soul. You know you have experienced true intimacy when you leave a person's presence, and your spirit and soul have been satisfied with little to no thought of gratification to the flesh. True intimacy causes productivity in the spirit and births something in the natural.

Relating in a healthy way causes attraction to develop into intimacy. That intimacy grows into deeply committed love. That love fosters attraction creating a lifelong cycle that repeats and is able to withstand the highs and lows of life.

8

PRINCIPLE 8
LOVE THE WAY GOD INTENDED

God is love. God created love. God made us in a fashion that we have a need for love as well as a need to love. Healthy relationships require us to have an understanding of love through God's eyes. Below are the answers to some questions I've been asked that I believe will help us gain a better understanding of love and to give and receive the love God intended.

Some say love is an action word. Some say love is an emotion or feeling. Some say sex is love. However, if we want to love the way God intended, we must examine what the Bible tells us love is. The NIV version of 1 Corinthians 13 describes love as being the following:

1. Longsuffering
2. Patient

3. Kind
4. Does not Envy
5. Does not Boast
6. Is not Proud
7. Does not dishonor other
8. Is not self-seeking
9. Is not easily angered
10. Keeps no record of wrongs
11. Does not delight in evil
12. Rejoices in good
13. Always protects
14. Always trusts
15. Always hopes
16. Always preserves
17. Never fails

I use 1 Corinthians 13 as a guide. I consider if the actions of this person are in line with God's definition of love. It will be difficult for a person who is not familiar with or hasn't experienced love displayed in this way to love you in this way. I also ask myself are my actions lining up with this Scripture.

I make a love Y Chart. You take a blank piece of pay and draw a big Y in the middle. On one leg, you put "looks like." On another, you put "feels like." On the last, you put "sounds like." You then record what love or one of its descriptors looks like, sounds like, and feels like to you. For example, Trust looks like me not going through your phone. Trust feels peaceful. Trust sounds confident.

God is the example of love. You can recognize love when you see god-like characteristics in people. For example, God loved, and he gave his best. When someone loves you, they give their best. So, how do I love the way God intended?

- Be willing to love from all the places God instructed us to love from. We are to love from our heart (emotional), soul (spiritual), mind (practical), and strength (physical).

- Be the love God intended — don't expect from other people what you are not willing to give. Work on your love walk. Ask people how they want to be loved and then be intentional about loving them in that manner.

- Receive the love God intended. This starts with receiving God's love. Then you must love yourself. Most people's inability to receive love stems from the fact that they don't believe they are worthy of the type of love God desires them to have.

Following are a few poems about the love God intended. Read them and allow them to minister to you.

Picture Perfect

The picture they paint of me is not correct. I'm not schizophrenic, and I don't have turrets. I'm not up down nor hot then cold. I don't yell, fight, cuss, and scold. I won't beat to a pulp. I don't give bruises and lumps. I don't use you to satisfy my need, fulfill my lust, or spread my greed.

I don't control your decisions by making threats. I don't use, abuse, or make you regret the day you met me or fell into my trap. I don't set out to deceive or make your emotions take a nap putting you to sleep in my lap.

I don't intentionally cause grief or bring you pain. I don't control your every move or make you feel ashamed of your walk, your talk, your dress, looks, or life. I am not your main source of misery or strife.

I won't isolate you, degrade you, cheat on you, never upgrade you; because to me, you are a treasure fearfully and wonderfully made so uniquely beautiful, there could never be an upgrade for you.

You SEE, when I am true, I am patient and kind, and when you mess up, I'm not quick to remind you of your faults because I see your need, so I cover and protect both you and seed.

I'M NOT JEALOUS, so I encourage you to be all you can be; I'll display your accomplishments for all the world to see. I'm into you, so by your side, I will stay. I'm in this forever, so come what may.

I'M NOT SELFISH, so I honor, respect, and put you first, and on your finger, I put a ring before I go up your skirt. I believe in you, want the best for you, and for you, I will bear all. I never fail, so you can trust me; I'll pick you up when you fall, be there when you call, won't procrastinate or stall, tear you down, or make you feel small.

You SEE, the picture they paint of me is just not true. My name is love, and I desire to meet you.

Love's Cry

Love's cry is to know you. Love's cry is to show you. Love's cry is to hold you. Love's cry is to mold you. Love's cry is to mend you. Love's cry is to send you into a lost and dying world.

LOVE IS CRYING out for you, yes you. Bring love your hurt. Bring love your pain. Bring love your loss and all of your shame. Love is crying out for you, yes you with all of your hang-ups and all of your mistakes, all of your failures in every move you make. Love cries out for you to receive love, believe in love, learn love, and be love.

LOVE'S MIND is constantly thinking of you. Loves eyes see the potential in you. Loves ears hear what you do and don't say. Loves heart longs for you every day. Loves mouth speaks positively into your life. Love's arms squeeze and hold you tight. Loves hands help you and take care of your needs and loves legs walk beside you into destiny.

LOVE IS CRYING out for you, yes you. Its cry is to know you, show you, shape, make, and mold you. To mend you, to send you into a lost and dying world. Love is crying out for you, yes you! The question is, will you answer?

Rejections Story: Ezekiel 16

My beloved, I handpicked you and gave you a wonderful life.

And in turn, you have proven an adulterous wife.

When I found you, no one pitied you. You were rejected and despised.

Left for dead in your own blood, you really should have died.

But in love, I saw your beauty, made you my everything, gave you all my love,

Gave you clothing, food, and shelter- let you lay on my rugs,

Sleep in my beds, eat at my table, It was you I made my queen

having been rejected, you could not receive my love, so very little did it mean

You turned your back on me, looked to others for love, and constantly flirted with sin.

I am your King, your Lover, your Lord, yet you take pleasure worshipping men.

Having other gods before me, you're stubborn and proud, murdering my children, yes, it's true.

And as if that's not enough, you solicit lovers and pay your patrons with the things I gave you.

It's Judgment time, so I look away as your lovers gather, and you are mocked and scorned.

Yes, I, your lover, look away as my love is cut with weapons and burned.

My love, your idolatry made me jealous; you'll be chastened sore but not left for dead.

I'll keep my covenant with you, but memories of this whipping will remain in your head.

My beloved, I handpicked you and gave you a wonderful life.

And in turn, My beloved, you have proven an adulterous life.

FINAL THOUGHTS

Relating in a healthy way requires intentionality, dedication, flexibility, making some tough decisions, and moving in them. I always say a decision not moved in is a decision not made.

Decide today to love the Lord, your God, with all your heart, soul, mind, and strength — and to love yourself enough to work on you and receive the love God desires you to have.

Happy Relating!

www.ingramcontent.com/pod-product-compliance
Lightning Source LLC
LaVergne TN
LVHW051513070426
835507LV00022B/3081